CAREER TALKS IN VERSES

Celebrating some Heroes of our Time

CAREER TALKS IN VERSES

Celebrating some Heroes of our Time

Onye Kingsley

ATHENA PRESS
LONDON

CAREER TALKS IN VERSES
Celebrating some Heroes of our Time
Copyright © Onye Kingsley 2007

ISBN 10-digit: 1 84401 861 X
ISBN 13-digit: 978 1 84401 861 1

First Published 2007 by
ATHENA PRESS
Queen's House, 2 Holly Road
Twickenham TW1 4EG
United Kingdom

Printed for Athena Press

*To my Chioma, the children,
and the young adults of our generation*

The author would like to thank the following people: David Moore, Thomas Mathew, Mark Sykes, and the editorial team and staff of Athena press for their immense help in the preparation of this book.

Thanks once again to you all.

KINGSLEY ONYE

Contents

Part Two

Part Three

Preface

These poems were borne out of the desire to help the younger generations in choosing a career. They are intended to give an insight and prompt them to ask questions and seek answers in making up their minds in career selection. Here all careers are projected to be rewarding, both financially and otherwise, but all have one thing in common: hard work. That's the only true road to success.

Part One
The Poems

Politicians/Statesmanship
Tribute to Nelson (Madiba) Mandela

Precarious terrain, which most dare not tread, except men of iron and steel, endowed with heroic blood from birth. The daredevils of positivity, of winds of change, of sweeping changes, come what may.

Willing scapegoats for others; the sacrificial lambs of nations in evil political quagmires and quandaries. Ready to die or live for a just cause and the dignity of oppressed mankind; ready to lose his own head while others are saving theirs.

Seriously focused, yet undaunted, even in the sure face of death. Daring to fight death in his own home, yet defenceless, save for the weapons of truth, principles and commitment to the cause he believes in: liberation of the deprived masses.

He never gave a hoot when the first carrot was dangled in his face; the tempting price of freedom, like the apple of knowledge in the Garden of Eden. There he proved himself a colossus, a man among men. Even the prison walls of Robben Island couldn't stop him.

At the end of the day, when the storm and the cloud clears, the truth wins the day; it wears the crown and reigns supreme, bringing peace to the peaceless, hope to the hopeless, life to the lifeless, victory to the victims, sanity to the insane.

Democracy and true freedom come to the deprived, bringing sunshine, once again to the old nations in darkness. This noble calling gets the thumbs up from history.

Presenters

Dedicated to Oprah Winfrey

Millions of troubled souls, bodies and spirits in captivity for ages without end, at last have a shoulder to cry on and pour out all their grief: those horrible life encounters, experiences, endless traumas, unfathomable nightmares...

Ever chasing our pasts, presents and futures; we look them in the face then lay them naked in the view of millions, unmasking the monsters of our lives in the quest for therapeutic answers and solutions.

As a good listener, the audience runs through the noble contents, searching for fitting and palliative answers and lasting solutions for the world's haunted souls, leaving no stone unturned. Neither kings nor queens,

Princesses nor princes are spared in this quest for truth to relieve and pacify the burdens of the troubled bodies, souls and spirits of this world. Relieved, with smiles on their faces, they can't give thanks enough to see those horrible nightmares disappear like the wind by the power of a promising dawn that ushers in bright sunlight at the end of their previous tunnel of darkness.

The Police

Dedicated to law enforcement officers the world over

L ives and properties at my charge; the masses in the country;

My duty is to protect. Criminals are cowed at the sight of me.

Like a shield, the law's behind me. The world could go to sleep like

A baby under its mother's care. Friend of all; enemy of crime

And perpetrators, who must be brought to book, with connections

In high places. Notwithstanding, the rule of law seeks them out.

My uniform is my identity, my government's pride.

Obey the law and be my friend.

Horticulturist

Dedicated to Alan Titchmarsh

L ove of nature is my propelling force, day and night.
Colours to blend from pot to pot, garden to garden.
Growing flowers is my stock in trade, and
Seed-tending from nursery to flowerbed.

Flowers of all kinds I nurture, as God takes care of us.
Growing plants from infancy to adulthood, with the right
soil,
Plenty of water and sunlight, I get the best from
Flowers, with colours that beat the imagination.

Nature's gift we shall strive to maintain.
Give and take is nature's law. Oxygen and carbon
Dioxide strive to exchange places.
What imagination could beat the love of nature?

Chef (Caterer)

Dedicated to Ainsley Harriott

S potless like the snow is my daily garb from kitchen to
  dining room:
My areas of influence. Nutrients; reasonably combined to
Match your diet; balanced or checked. Little wonder you
  grow
Healthy and blooming each day, thanks to my job in the
  kitchen.

Kings and subjects alike are at my beck and call. At
  celebration time
I feed thousands at important functions,
Shaking hands with leaders, kings and queens for a job
Well done. They don't forget my service.

I know they all call again when occasion demands.
I prance up and down joyfully, like a little kitten in
A basket, clutching my cheque, smiling to the bank and
Thanking God for this noble profession.

Medical Doctor

Dedicated to medical professionals the world over

H ale and hearty are my watchwords. At your beck and
call
When you're indisposed, my sure-fire treatment saves you.
Proud to walk around my neighbourhood, I know
I can cure ailments. No one prescribes drugs in my absence.

Patients must queue to hear my word, the word that spells
Doom to ailments of all kinds. As white as snow,
My uniform endears me to all and sundry. An apple every
Day keeps me away from you. My job is not for a lazy mind.

Like a clock, I work around the day, knowing delays could
Lead to the deaths of thousands. Like an armour bearer,
I brace myself for my onerous task, accepting all it
Takes to remain in the profession of a medical doctor.

Farmer

Widespread land is my ultimate pleasure; growing
    Crops, line by line – rice, beans, others – my subject
  matter.
Using machines on virgin sites, I clear them of weeds and
  plants;
Overgrown fields are my first fields, and my first stage.

I create ridges and mounds for my first preparation,
Thanking my tractor for obedience to orders. Planting,
I apply fertiliser and hope for the glorious touch of Mother
Nature, brightened with the smiling face of the sun that
  shines

To soothe our worthy countenance. Up they spring,
Seeds earlier planted. Nature and I, in concert,
Struggle daily to make an arduous harvest.
Days run into weeks; weeks into months.

Harvesting time, we announce, an arduous time indeed.
That journey between the market and home
To the kitchen, and finally from your dining table to your
  stomach,
Keeping you hale and healthy. What a lovely job, my job.

Pilot

Dedicated to all those who suffered in the 11 September tragedies

Transatlantic trips were once a mirage. Now they're a
reality.
Smiling, with compass to hand, I am hooked to the
Cockpit of an Airbus, with several lives and
Properties on board, wholly at my trust.

A little turbulence could ruin it all. God is by my side with
Experience and expertise;
Together we enjoy the mystery of birds in the sky
Beyond the reach of your fingertips,
Even when on tiptoes, stretching to a breaking point.

High above, beyond Mother Earth,
Seas, trees and mountains are far below.
Here I'll be slugging it out with the wind, clouds and
Thunderstorms, matching might with might, the tale

Of man's dominion over creation,
Till my burden is gently lowered to the
Tarmac as I land on the runway,
Bearing good fortune and praise.

Journalist

Dedicated to the BBC/CNN

A newshound, that Jack-of-all-trades from coast to
coast:
Ears alert, pen handy, with papers to scratch.
Whatever goes, my interest burns, burning for

Facts and figures to hit the front page, the TV and news-stands.
Competition is rife as reporters stumble upon
Themselves in dissemination of news through the media –

Complex networks, far and near.
Troubled zones are our hot cakes; I risk
My single life as if there were duplicates.
Microphones are our close associates. We serve it hot

On TV screens and pages of newspapers,
Dragging the whole wide world to your doorsteps
Without batting an eyelid nor setting a foot outside,
And reeling off the news that could make or mar your day.

Artist

Dedicated to Pablo Picasso

C lose to nature, my daily drill: semblance
Structures. My hands conjure. Obeisant to nature,
I see her as the first in this field of creativity.

My work is to put my whole being on paper
Without benefit of a doubt.
I touch areas of your life, like the
Patterns on your clothes inspire the painting of a house.

For the Picassos and Jacksons of this world,
An infinite legacy endures long, long
After our demise and cuts across class and creed.

Mechanic

Dedicated to all mechanics

C omplex networks, mechanical intricacies are my
crosswords;
Our game. Perfect ordering of your wares sets
Even your automobiles in neat assemblage.
Like a physician I feel their pulse, apply normal medication,

Bring them back to life to follow suit with their peers.
My attire: an overall with a helmet, boots and spanners
To match, a far cry from my box of tools; with tools intact,
All set, I surge forward to treat mechanical ailments.

Your computer a drop in the ocean
Of your electronic appliances. I make and cure them,
Once again bringing civilisation to your doorstep.
This is my noble job.

Miner/Driller

Dedicated to all oil explorers and treasure hunters the world over

N ature's hidden wealth it's my lot to discover
And turn around. Far beneath Mother
Earth, there they are, in innumerable quantities
And qualities in land and sea, even rocks.

Like a masquerade: I mask myself from possible harm;
One cannot be too sure. Miles and miles I drill beneath
The earth as I thirst to lay my hands on them:
Those treasures, hidden out of sight but
Not out of mind by Mother Nature.

Luck on my side, my nation smiles as
Nations fall over nations in a bid to strike deals with it.
Deals are made that better the lot of my people as
Our reserves and revenues soar to high heaven,
Touching the numerous lives of the underprivileged
For the better; this is my legacy to mankind.

Lawyer

Justice and fair play are my watchwords,
My noble course is the rule of law
At all levels;
At all costs it must be upheld.

Never mind whose ox is gored; connection in high places
A vain attempt, as justice delayed is as not denied.
As a lion, hungry for prey, so I hunger
For justice and equity for the cheated.

On consultation I turn on the heat, ransacking my law
books.
The constitution is our veritable weapon on our battlefield –
The law courts – where none is more equal than others.

Fashion Designers

Tribute to the late Giovanni Versace

My clothes make you look
Like a movie star, you may think.
Of course, my clients are lined up from Hollywood to
Monte Carlo. My handiwork shines,
My designs.

Desperate for good or weird looks, stars storm up,
Stumbling over my designs with huge sums, huge ideas.
Crazed, I get down to work, coordinating men,
Materials and machines, with a dexterity that makes
You green with envy.

I transform your outward countenance;
Fans fall head over heels as they queue
Endlessly for my autograph.

Banker

Heavily decked out, like a cricket in October, clean-
shaven or bearded,
With a tie to match, ready for the day's business,
All set to check facts and figures with a computer,
My best friend at the touch of buttons.

Accountability is my watchword as I coordinate
Your monetary affairs, making it my business,
My daily bread.

Customers come; some leave, itching to have
My word as projects linger on for finances unfunded.
Taking my time, with utmost care, I choose
The feasibility and viability of projects. This becomes

My propelling force, whilst collateral becomes
My backbone and struggles with the rest to strike
A balance, in a bid to float or sink

In the unpredictable business world of today.
Reasonable risks, taken to ensure
My success; how I love my trade!

Postmasters

Tribute to the Royal Mail

Your burden's my burden as I race to deliver
Your parcels and mail. The contents are not my business
As I comb countries and nations to get across
Your message – good or bad.

Like a guard, a watchdog, I ensure your mail's
Delivered into the right hands. My single stride covers the
Crannies and nooks bearing your news, bitter and sweet.
Done with, I hurry to my station like an obedient servant

In his master's employ. Bearing good fruit attracts
High remuneration in cash and kind to better my lot.
How miserable life could have been without my job!

Sailor

Floating on the seas, my lovely castle with countless cabins,
Journeys from coast to coast on the high seas.
My neighbours in this world mingle with the heavens
When perceived afar. At my fingertips:

My lovely castle, with those aboard my duty to direct,
Compass in sight. Safety for all, like Noah's Ark.
For weeks and weeks, we sail on the high seas,
Till the next port of call to berth. Like enraged bull,

The storms attack me, undeterred even when
I've anchored to rest my nerves.
Like troublesome children, they tug at my lovely castle –
Oh, my castle.

Salesman

B est of friends to manufacturers of varied products
Of kinds and brands, as I get to the marketplace,
   introducing them,
As I will, my neighbours to my best friends.

Armed with field strategies, marketing every claim
And counter-claim as sales reps hang at each other's throats in
Desperate bids for fast and high sales,
You can bet it, I'll sell coals in Newcastle.

As I saunter like a warrior of words with verbal strategies,
My targets, my clients, are convinced as
I encourage them not to look at price tags,
But glory in the benefits of the products for their lives.

Hooked on my words, clients troop in, crowding to buy
My products. Overwhelmed with joy, I hurry home,
With pockets filled; my commission is the
Sweet reward of my toil, my job.

Film Actors/Producers

Tribute to Steven Spielberg

I dream of the perfection of the arts and of acting.
I read over scripts, desperate to master
All my lines to the letter, actions and speeches, even sounds.
Scouting all over the world, shopping for ideas,

Costumes and locations, I struggle in concert
To make imagination a reality, bringing dreams
To life for all to swallow hook, line and sinker.

I often succeed. Stars are born when
Mother Luck smiles on us, as we hit the box office
Topping the chart, bursting it, with the magic wand
Of success. Transcending fame to superstardom,

Opening doors and doors as money rolls in, touching
Our lives. My films reflect the innermost lives of my fans
Who cannot wait to get to the movies?

Athlete (Sprinter)

Tribute to Carl Lewis

My legs and might are my veritable weapons.
Like a hare, I spring to proximity, past milestones,
With an agile elegance carrying along all my being.

On the track, a single thought crosses
My mind: victory, the gold medal.
Nothing else. All must be put to the track.
Not silver, nor bronze – it's gold or nothing.

My spirit is sportsmanship.
As I fly on the track, toes barely touching the ground,
Hands swift like an eagle's wings.

I don't care who's tailing – looking back is out
Of the question, till my chest hits the ribbons as the
Judges declare me winner.

Even on success, doors open to touch the lives
Of my nation, kith and kin, all for the better,
Like fresh water from the morning spring.
I love this race!

Basketball Player

Tribute to Michael Jordan

Hopping from spot to spot, bouncing my orange ball,
Set to spring surprises as I launch for the basket,
Desperate for dunks, some good ones.

My height and dexterous moves an edge over my peers as
I fly in the sky to shoot for goal.
Like a prankster, goal-oriented,
I duck and twist,
Charging like an enraged bull,

Ball in hand, slam-dunking right into the basket.
Distance and height are never an issue as I hit my target
Like an archer with a quiverful of arrows, aiming for
The bull's eye and hitting it.

Nurse

Tribute to the nurses of this world

C are of patients is my guiding call.
Like a butterfly on flowers, I stay with them,
Never wanting to let them alone to suffer in the
Cruel hands of solemn thoughts and ailments.

Daily medication it's my duty to administer with the
Utmost care, which makes them cry for joy.
I give them enough reasons to hang on to life
And beloved ones, I tell them of Jesus' love for children.

Their pulse and temperature it's my duty to check
And take records, a step-by-step account of recuperation
From the shackles of illness and possible death to

The haven of liberty that is good health,
The happiest home of all.
My wonderful job – how I love it!

Teacher

Tribute to teachers of this world

L ike a potter I took up the challenge,
Making the school my potter's wheel and children's
minds my clay.
Love for kids is my first weapon as I
Stealthily enter their minds like a

Thief in the night. They are spellbound as
I get their attention and ears.
Taking time to lead them through my tutelage

And good education, a veritable instrument for a better
tomorrow.
Societal decorum is my place of emphasis as
Parents join hands in provision of their own teaching.

Society stands to be better off with goal-oriented
Adults that make nations go places and this world a better
place.
My noble profession: oldest, but newest.

Singer

Tribute to Lionel Ritchie

E ntertainment is my stock in trade.
I could sing from dusk till dawn,
Bringing those sounds that kill your sorrows,
Heal your souls, bringing you to a wholesome

Rebirth and regeneration.
My golden voice touches the heart of hearts,
And knows no bound as instruments, like spice,
Add to its taste and flavour.

Angels from heaven nod their heads rhythmically to savour
The pleasing tune of my renditions,
Causing my solemn star to shine to stardom.
The product of my hard work is talent admired by Almighty
   God.

Clergy

Tribute to all men of God, with due respect to other faiths

S alvation's message is my noble call.
Good news to all, I preach my sermon on the mountains,
Nooks and crannies to all lands and clans.

The Holy Bible is my reference point.
Jesus taught us the greatest love of all,
Hanging there, on the cross of Calvary, infallible and
Just, for your sake and mine,

That we might be saved.
As I ascend the pulpit to bear testimony to this truth
I know the world knew but hated to hear.
I recall Christ's mission

On earth, unfolding mysteries, ministries and the
Healing power of the only begotten Son of God Almighty,
Our Rock of Ages.

Astronaut

Dedicated to the astronauts of this world

Visiting the galaxies; space exploration.
Launch the rocket, my transporter, my spaceship.
Millions of miles are covered in the twinkling of an eye.
At an incredible speed.

The moon is a friendly spot; familiar terrain;
Haven't found courage enough to visit others.
I am heavily dressed to protect
My body from possible harm,
Unpredictable gases and radioactivity.

Bon voyage! I place my nation's flag on the moon,
Fixing the satellite to cover the whole wide world,
As I float back and forth like a balloon in the wind.
With little care of the
Mortal danger I'm letting myself into.

Meteorologist

Dedicated to Michael Fish

C onscious of time, my sphere of duty is the
Weather forecast, my joy of joys.
I undertake experiments and tests for accuracy,
Prompting me to give details on how and
When it might fall – rain, of course. I can give you a

Pre-situational idea to help your timing, programmes
And schedules as the day breaks.
Conscious of these, I can't be caught with my pants down
As time is taken to arrange things to suit your needs.
Rain or shine; bright or dull.
Which way? The weather picks.
I'll be there to tell you.

Builder (Civil Engineer)

Complex shelters: mansions, towers and skyscrapers are all
My handiwork. My brainchild.
I sit down to plan. My drawing board is a veritable
Weapon as I co-ordinate men, machines and

Materials for works according to my blueprints,
Not missing a dot. Off to a site, my
Feet in boots, helmet on head, with glove-covered hands,
I join in, barking out orders in a desperate

Bid to transform drawings to physical structures.
I make dreams a reality as tenants move
In to shelter bodies and souls,
Thanking nature for my noble job.

Firefighter

Dedicated to fire brigades worldwide

L ittle sparks make an ocean of flames, a mighty
conflagration,
Messing up lives and properties,
Turning victims into balls of fire and smoke and
Ashes, for no just cause.

At a moment's notice, like a stuntman,
I leap into the fire engine, whizzing off to the
Location of the fire, the troubled spot.

I'm combat-ready, of course, with men and apparatus.
Firefighting is our quest.
Boldly armed to the teeth, brandishing the hosepipe
Long enough to break barriers,

We burst into rooms, up stairs, through ceilings, dealing
Deadly blows to daredevil flames. We teach fire to
Steer clear of people's lives, properties, wares and effects.
This is my noble calling.

Carpenter

Nature's vegetation, trees I hunt
Of varied species, types and kinds. I hunt
The forest to make my choice.

Having found one, purposefully brandishing
My saw like a woodchopper, down the tree goes.
I drag it to the factory. Dressed in my overalls with
Measuring tape and marker, I am ready for work,

Ready to saw. I use my tools to cut the timber to
Various sizes and shapes. I make the furniture
For your homes and offices; it is my handiwork, my pride.
My work leaves no trace in your mind that

It was once a living tree.
My job beats your imagination, leaving you green
With envy as I'm paid for my services.
I'm off to the bank with a smile on my face.

Dentist

Troubled teeth it's my duty to mend.
As bacteria drills holes into them, fighting tooth
And nail in a bid to damage them. The attack can
Hardly be seen with the naked eye.

Decay gathers on our teeth in
The course of mastication. Unwary of the danger
Inherent, we all sleep away like a baby in
Its cot

While bacteria comes to feed on the leftovers
Of the day before.
Rotten teeth are the resultant effects as we rush to the
Dentist to save our jaws from unspeakable pain.

Secretary

My boss's secret it's my duty to keep.
Files and documents, I must
Produce at the boss's request;
I know where each is kept.

Like a barometer, I measure the atmosphere, knowing
When he's happy or not.
Like a watchdog I protect him, barring unfriendly

Faces from view, even when I am nagged.
Like a travel agency, I prepare him to get out of town.
Like a computer, I run his outfit when he's not around.

Full of confidence, I can be trusted through thick
And thin. Lots of remuneration for me, when he's back –
A reward to a loyal employee, the boss's pride.

Playwright

Tribute to William Shakespeare

S cripts and speeches it's my calling to write,
As I pick up my pen to scratch the paper.
I put characters together in concert,
Fiction or non-fiction.

To achieve my aim, I depict true life,
The way it is, the way it ought to be.
Like a mirror, I reflect the truth in life people pretend to
  ignore.
Hitting them right in the face with real-life situations,

Prompting them to turn a new leaf,
Making this world a better place for all;
This is my enriching calling.

Shopkeeper

With a smile on my face, approvingly, I nod to customers
As they troop in and out, baskets in hand,
Marching along my stock-filled shelves, looking for things to
    buy,
Darting their eyes to and fro along my goods.

They check out brand names, labels and dates,
Struggling with themselves to make up their minds, bearing
In mind price tags,
Coming to terms with reasons,

They stretch their hands forth, putting the goods
Right into their basket. Basket filled,
They stroll to the cashier's counter to pay their bills,
And this is my sweet job.

Photographer (Paparazzi)

Tribute to Lady Diana, Princess of Wales

T he daily hunt for snapshots is my duty call. Personal,
Industrial and corporate shots my daily bread,
Solicited or not; who cares? Like a gamble,
Every shot goes, at times, to the detriment of targets,
Who often get ruined.
Hot chase, terrible obsession, when targets are superstars,
Personality profiles of note. For this feat, mums could be
Exchanged for a dime for us to have a shot.

Monetary gains are the propelling force,
As the media lays its hands on the pics. Good ones
Receive adequate compensation in cash and kind,
In defiance of conscience.

This world was robbed of her royal elegance in
Sartorial splendour at her prime of life.
Throwing away this ocean-milk of human kindness.
Methinks our job calls for caution and review in the future.

Veterinary Surgeon

B est of friends to animals, people's pets.
I feel their pulse to trace their ailments.
Since none can speak a word,
I take time to make discoveries, detecting

Their ailments through moods and mannerisms.
At times, physical defects could be a pointer.
I could apply general vaccines to boot.

Out massive deaths among poultry! I save them and
Their owners from the pain of loss
My lovely job.

Footballer

Tribute to Pele

R ight on the green, green grass field,
   Dressed in jersey with boots to match, ball at the
   centre.
Ready for kicks; eleven against eleven;
A war of might, experience and tact.

Attack and defence is our noble course,
With obedience to rules. The highest score of goals
Declares the winner with countless goodies.

Fired by talents, training and long-sufferings,
Coupled with the thirst for goals, more goals.
Like a charging bull, broken away from its tether,
I dash for the ball, dribbling, twisting and beating opponents

One after another, gunning for box eighteen, the
Goalpost – my target. As I push towards the goal-
Keeper, I give him the false hope of catching the ball
And stopping a lone goal.

My shot like a thunderbolt takes the net apart
In unspeakable mechanical daze. Coast clears;
There lies a goalkeeper at the tail wing of his post,
Buried in self-pity as he wonders. What a goal.

Milkman

From doorstep to doorstep, the white juice of life is
My duty to vend to all and sundry; to every nook and
cranny.
The first food of creatures at birth and the cradle of life.
As children's cries indicate discomfort and wants,

Sets mums scampering for the pacification of their children
Who take solace in the warm sweet taste of
The running juice from mothers' breasts.
Insufficient from mother, we turn to cows

For supplement. Our bowls overflow their brims
Like a running river runs over banks.
Reaching all and sundry for sale and use;
This is my job.

Drivers

Dedicated to bus and public transport drivers

C ommuters' stress it's my stress to bear,
Commuters' burden it's my burden to bear,
Commuters' routes my duty to ply.
I drive from street to street, the

Highway road, and relevant routes to meet their needs.
Day in, day out, these things I do to put smiles on their
  faces.
Like the back of my hands,
I acquaint myself with their routes,
Taking people to and from their working places,

Friends and families; and bring in revenues
To the authorities that put things together to meet our
Endless needs and make our nation a proud one
Among equals.
This is my lovely job, which I cherish.

Electrician

'Let there be light: and there was light';
The biblical lines one never forgets.
Even the devil himself prefers light to darkness.
That's why you won our hearts,
A wonderful darling you are as you brighten our streets, homes,
Everywhere; you
Gave our electronics reason to serve us
Without blinking an eyelid, even our computers, communication
Systems of our media.
Houses, stage-setting and countless tasks you undertake on our behalf,
Leaving us with no excuse
But to give you the thumbs-up and V-signs, accolades
Worthy of your lovely job.

Clowns

Dedicated to Charlie Chaplin

T he sight of you melts away the burden in my heart.
   Even before you open your mouth to say something,
I'm almost dying of laughter.
The look of your oversized boots,
The look of your stuffy, overgrown coloured wigs,
The look of your bogus, multicoloured costume:
A sight that makes my day and checks my adrenaline.
This keeps me whole and hearty as all my troubles melt
   away;
As I behold you, it makes my day.
I rock with laughter and almost pee in my pants
Because of you.

Charity Fundraisers

Dedicated to Oxfam and the Red Cross

L ittle do you know how many
Lives you've saved.
Little do you know how many
Broken homes you've restored.
Little do you know how many of the
Hopeless you've given real hope
And will to carry on their lives.
Little do you know how many
Nobodies you've made somebodies.
Little do you know how many orphans
You've given home and families.
Little do you know how many of the poverty-
Stricken, you've given riches.
Little do you know how many
Tears you've stopped people from shedding
In the midst of misery and despondency.
If only you knew.
If only you knew.
You've got the best job
In the world, making it
A better place than you found it.

Chemist

Dedicated to scientists the world over

N ature's hidden roots, herbs and leaves,
     I sort these out and fashion them into medications.
Day after day there are new discoveries
As ailments grow in different forms.
Some could be resistant, I have
To solve the problem with a different
Sort of medication.
I work hard with the medical team
In my field to fashion drugs to cure your ailments and
Keep you whole through thick and thin,
As you jog around your
Neighbourhood with the utmost
Faith in your well-being.

Emergency Services Phone Operator

A stitch in time saves nine. That's
The best I can describe
Your noble job that
Keeps you on your toes at all times

Lest the worst happens, throwing
Panic into everyone.
A run of 999 distressed phone calls,

At any hour of the day, fires up the office, scrambling for
Every member of staff on duty. As you take down callers'
   names,
Incidents or accidents, addresses and directions,
Getting relevant staff alerted, up and on

To a noble cause of rescue operations.
Trailblazers they are, as they prove themselves
The true heroes of our time.
Your noble job is praiseworthy.

Comedians

Nature's natural gift of amusement is your sphere
Of influence as you chat to all and sundry,
Making their day as bright as possible.
Your comic talent comes to hand

As you make us rock with laughter.
Young and old, none is spared your jokes, even
Your team are not making it any easier
As you join hands to make our day

And shield us from the wicked, painful realities
Of this world and give us renewal, strength
And vigour to start a bright new day.
You save us from the wicked pangs of

High blood pressure and its likes in this world.
Millions praise you for your job that
Saves lives and makes our day.

Geologists

Dedicated to the Tsunami disaster victims

Various soils and landscapes, textures, mountains and valleys it's
My job to inspect and put to test any I find in good time
Before it is too late.
This I do to stem the effects

Of surprises – of natural disasters
Like volcanic eruptions, earthquakes, land tremors,
Landslides and the likes, even agricultural adventures.
I check the acidity of the soil, landscapes, rocks and mountains
Even beneath the sea, in oil explorations.

All these I cover to make this world's locations a safer place
For all to live in and cherish.

Zoologist

Dedicated to David Attenborough

K ind-hearted, my duty calls.
Thousands of animals on
Planet Earth I am duty bound to care for.
I study these species, matching

Each with their like and nature.
Their psychology and tendencies,
These I take in context with other things to
Come up with the finest ways to do my job.

I keep the world acquainted with each discovery
To save my friends, who can neither speak our language nor
 ask for favours.

Cobbler

Dedicated to chiropodists and cobblers of this world

C are of your feet: my lovely job.
I work endlessly in my factory shop

To make your day; measuring your feet and the
Choice leather, among other things, to put a smile on your
   face.
I shield your feet from the
Hazards of the road on which you

Tread for play, daily bread or
Walking your dogs. Fear not, for I've already
Helped to protect your feet, with beautiful

Designs in shoes that will leave you
Gobsmacked – my lovely job.

Plumber

Water pipes; drainage pipes: these are
Yours to sort, your lovely job
As you keep us safe from possible
Overflowing of our streets, kitchens, bathrooms,

Even bedrooms.
Perhaps we don't realise enough
The importance of your wonderful job
Unless we have a breakdown of
Our pipe water systems.

Then we nag you to do your best,
Mate, 'cos we know you've got the magic
Touch of the water emergency services.
Keep on keeping on at
Your noble job,
Which saves our day and keep us dry.
Thank you; thanks a lot.

Carer and Support Worker

The unspoken thoughts of a service user, dedicated to carers

Each time someone knocks at our door, I hope it's you.
The picture of you often comes, racing in my mind's eye.
I rush to the door, hoping my imaginings are true.

Those loving smiles and words you share with us,
Make our days. Even when we were at it, giving you hell
You never asked for. The greatest challenge of your life,
Pushing your endurance almost to breaking point.

Even then, you are still our friend, full of smiles with patience
And tolerance. Little do you know how we appreciate these
Wonderful, kind gestures you offer; this understanding...
If we could call it that.

We cherish your loving support and try to make it up to you
    by promoting
Our independence, doing certain things ourselves, reducing
    your
Burden, knowing we can't do it all alone. Nevertheless, we
    give you
Thanks: thanks a lot, even though you can't hear us well
    enough.

But our eyes and body language say it all, because it's you and only,

You alone can understand these unspoken thoughts in our minds.

The British Navy and Sea Britain

Dedicated to the British Royal Navy (one of the best in the world)

Sea Britain; massive volumes; awe-inspiring.

Liquid warrior; salty wizards; fighting demons – that's what you are

As you battle your embankments, sea shores, with painful splash of your salty waters.

Eating up rocks, sandy beaches and mighty wave-mountains, which have the misfortune of crossing your paths.

If not for you, since medieval till date, how could we have visited other nations of the world, drunk purified water?

Feed our seabirds, water our farms, do our fishing, make discoveries,

Fight our battles and call the shots that proved our greatness that ruled the world in those days,

Not to mention the transportation opportunities you've afforded

Us, since the beginning of time.

Your battle-ready waves and dead weights float our ships,
ferries, boats, not to talk
Of our royal warships and submarines.
Marines and naval expeditions you made us proud of.
For us, you are the secret champion of our victories.

Each time we look at you, we cannot but wonder at your
source
Of strength and inner potential, some of which we are yet
to discover and pride
Upon, hoping you'll let us into this little secret of yours, as
you made Great Britain truly great.

Security Officer

There I'll stand, hours on end,
At the entrance of your shops,
Your living quarters, my business premises.
My job is to protect and guard, keeping

Unwelcome visitors away.
My watchful eyes are like those of the eagles.
On a bright summer morning, as I patrol
Your premises, I dart eyes around, to protect

Your interests from the dubious-minded intruders
Who often plague your sites with ulterior motives,
Pretending to be friends; but wolves in sheep's clothing,
That's what they really are.

Armed with my training, radio phone and my torch,
I make their dreams a nightmare as I expose their
Motives and hand them over into the hands of the law
Enforcers, whose job it is to bring them to book at the
Law courts; their painful rewards
Are reaped where they do not sow.

The Bin Man

Dedicated to all bin men and environmentalists of our time

From twilight to sunshine,
Your rubbish is mine to clear and sort out.
Journeying from north to south, east to west,
I derive my joy from that, hoping you'll understand

How much I care about your surrounding and well-being,
At present and for the future.
I struggle to keep bacteria and disease well away
From you and your family,

Leaving you to wonder how much I risk my health,
Bracing the biting cold of the winter morning,
Not to talk of the steaming hot sunshine of the summer

To sort your bins, your dirt, and save lives of millions from possible infections, epidemic out-breaks and pollution that could have sent millions of people to their early graves, leaving their homes desolate. My lovely job, which seems the lowest but is the greatest, if you know what I mean!

Part Two

Explanation of the Poems

Politician/Statesman

The poet celebrates the inner ability of great men in politics, who are able to make the world and people around them better than they found it, those who selflessly serve their nation and are even ready to pay the supreme sacrifice for the noble cause they believe in. These are men who could liberate and better the lot of their nations, men of iron and steel, endowed with heroic blood from birth. According to the poet, these men are the real political messiahs of mankind.

Presenters

Reference is made to all presenters, especially the ones that deal with problematic real-life issues of the people.

The poet celebrates in awe the ability of a total stranger (the presenter) to get people to trust them enough to pour out their hearts to them, even their greatest secrets, exposed on camera for millions to view worldwide. Such a wonderful level of trust is celebrated by the poet. These people are good listeners, searching for fitting and palliative answers and lasting solutions to the 'world's haunted souls'.

The Police

The poet is trying to explain the job of police officers as regards the protection of lives and properties of the citizens.

He makes it clear that the police befriend people who are law-abiding. Lawbreakers are the policeman's enemies who must be brought to book, connection in high places notwithstanding.

Horticulturist

The poet celebrates the job of horticulturists: how they tend flowers from the beginning to maturity, like Jesus takes care of us. He further mentions how plants take in carbon dioxide while giving us oxygen. This he refers to as the love of nature.

Chef (Caterer)

Celebrating the cleanness and neatness of the chef's uniform, the poet describes how he combines various ingredients and to create a good dish for his patrons. The chef prepares food for the high and mighty in this society, and he ends up with fat cheques to bank.

Medical Doctor

The poet describes the diligence of a medical doctor as he treats patients' ailments and prescribed medicines for them: 'Patients must queue to hear my word'. He dignifies the medical profession as doctors and GPs work diligently around the clock to save lives. He further makes it clear how difficult the job is.

Farmer

A depiction of the pleasure a farmer derives from his job, running through all the stages of farming: clearing of weeds, creation of ridges, planting, tending and finally harvesting.

The poet further celebrates how nature supports him to realise a good harvest: good weather encourages the plants or crops to do well in the soil. And last of all the farmer ensures we are all well fed. The harvested crops journey to your markets, homes, kitchens, and so to your dining table and stomach, keeping you healthy.

Pilot

The poet expresses surprise at the mystery of man in the sky, the wonder of flying a huge machine like an aeroplane in the quest for trips all over the globe. Great responsibility goes with this job: several lives and their property are on board. The job needs a great deal of experience and expertise. The poet further celebrates the altitude an aeroplane can reach ('Here I'll be slugging it out with the wind, clouds and thunderstorms.') He finally points out man's dominion over creation: not even birds could fly to that height. He further stresses the importance of safe landing for the pilot.

Journalist

The poet celebrates the important job of a journalist and people working in the mass media and how they go around hunting for news items.

He explains the most difficult aspects of the job: journalists risk their lives to cover news in trouble zones of the globe, e.g. the Iraq war. They take these risks, sometimes at the cost of their lives, just to bring us the latest news on the media network – what a good job!

Artist

The closeness of the artist to Mother Nature is celebrated by the poet in the world of creativity. He explains that the work of creativity endures for ever.

Mechanic

The poet celebrates the numerous works of mechanics worldwide. He makes us aware of the existence of different fields; he celebrates all of them in one breath, explaining how a mechanic prides himself as master of his field.

Miner/Driller

The natural mineral resources of the world are celebrated by the poet, and more so the miners or drillers who discover them. These professionals not only discover these minerals but also turn them to our good use, e.g. crude oil for petroleum products, gas, raw gold dust into finished goods, etc. Even diamonds are finely cut among others. The praise goes to the miners who discover them.

Lawyer

The poet here admires the fairness and fair play of honourable lawyers in running their jobs, obeying the rule of law, upholding it by making use of the constitution to protect and defend people's rights and privileges.

Fashion Designers

The poet celebrates the admirable works of fashion designers the world over as they help others with the current trend in fashions. He describes how fashion designers come out with beautiful designs that make us proud.

Banker

The poet celebrates the enviable work of the bankers as they dress up in dark suits, ready for work. He admires the principle of accountability, what they bring to bear on their field, and how they help to ensure profitable ventures and help thousands who are not able to sort their finances themselves.

Postmasters

The poet celebrates the wonderful work of the postmasters as they deliver people's parcels and mail from one destination to another, all around the globe. He appreciates how they cover the entire world with their deliveries and how they seem to love their job.

Sailors

The sailor's ship is referred to as a 'lovely castle with countless cabins'. The poet further admires how the sailor travels from coast to coast on the oceans of this world. He refers to the oceans as his neighbours because of the long time the sailor often spends on seas navigating, using his compass. The poet makes a biblical reference to Noah's Ark as a symbol of safety. He further makes mention of the terrific power of storms at sea and how they 'tug at my lovely castle'.

Salesman

The business acumen of a salesman is discussed, as he is seen as the manufacturers' best friend, creating markets for products and services. 'You can bet it, I'll sell coals in Newcastle,' claims the salesman, armed 'with verbal strategies'. He is able to convince customers to buy his wares.

Film Actors/Producers

The beautiful world of actors, actress and producers in the film world is celebrated by the poet as he admires their creative potential. They tour the world, shopping for ideas, customers and locations, 'to make imagination a reality, bringing dreams to life for all to swallow hook, line and sinker.' Their overall success opens doors to many others, creating jobs, and millions of lives take a turn for the better.

Athlete (Sprinter)

This poem describes the strength of an athlete and the spirit of sportsmanship. The poet lays emphasis on how focused a sprinter is whenever he is on the track for a race: he doesn't stop until he wins. It's gold or nothing. They have victory in mind at the start of any race: the spirit of a good sportsman.

Basketball Player

The agility of the basketball player is admired by the poet. The narrator tells us he is often 'set to spring surprises as I launch for the basket.' The poet points out that the height of a basketball player is an advantage for successful goal-scoring.

Nurse

The poet adores the noble job of all people in the nursing field, including carers and all others aiding the medical profession. He appreciates their hard work and love, and their care for the sick and disabled. They nurture them to health, 'the haven of liberty… The happiest home of all.'

Teacher

Describing the teacher as a potter and the learners as clay, the poet commends the wonderful work of teachers as a good role model for youngsters and 'a veritable instrument for a better tomorrow.' He finally posits that parents join hands with teachers to mould children into tomorrow's good, successful and responsible adults, making their society a proud one. He sees teaching as noble profession – 'oldest but newest.'

Singer

The poet celebrates the wonderful talent of a singer, saying that songs heal a person's soul, bringing people to a wholesome rebirth and regeneration. He attests that angels nod their heads rhythmically to savour the pleasing tune of human song. He further notes that the singer's voice is the product of real hard work.

Clergy

The clergy bring the Christian faith and the message of salvation to believers, using the Holy Bible as their reference material. Biblical illustration is made of Jesus Christ hanging on the cross of Calvary, infallible, for your sake and mine.

The poet makes reference to the Christian message of Christ's mission on earth.

Astronaut

The poet celebrates the works of the astronauts as they embark on space exploration, using different makes of rockets to cover millions of miles with incredible speeds. The moon is a friendly spot and familiar terrain for the astronauts, who need courage to visit the planets. He describes the movement of the astronauts in space especially on the moon.

Meteorologist

The poet celebrates the ability of the meteorologists to determine the day's weather, helping everyone to plan their days without surprises.

Builder (Civil Engineer)

The poet celebrates the importance of the job of builders and civil engineers: their ability to erect and construct complex shelters, mansions and skyscrapers. The poet admires how the builders transform the drawing of an architect into a real building with wonderful aesthetics.

Firefighter

The poet celebrates the noble job of the firefighters, how they are brave and courageous enough to put out mighty fires as soon as they start at whatever location. They move in like a bunch of stuntmen, 'combat-ready'.

Carpenter

A celebration of how a whole tree, with leaves, is chopped down and converted into furniture and other uses by the carpenters. Great intelligence lies behind this creativity. The poet also observes that by the time the tree trunks are put into finished products one can hardly recognise the fact that it was once a healthy living tree with leaves and branches. A lot of money lies in furniture-making.

Dentist

The wonderful profession of a dentist is celebrated here by the poet. He reminds us of the causes of tooth decay.

Secretary

The wonderful work of a secretary is celebrated by the poet. He further acknowledges the sensitive nature of a secretary: 'Like a barometer, I measure the atmosphere, his pulse knowing when (boss is) happy or not.' The poet rounds off by depicting the confidence the boss has in his secretary, and that brings good fortune to the secretary.

Playwright

A celebration of playwrights' wonderful creative abilities. The poet elaborates on the importance of the job of a playwright, depicting true life the way it is. He concludes that the playwright does this to make this world a better place for all.

Shopkeeper

The poet celebrates the wonderful job of merchandising as supermarkets and others help people to meet their daily needs by providing goods for sale.

Photographer (Paparazzi)

A celebration of the wonderful work of photographers as they capture images of the world just the way it is for records, safe-keeping and adoration, if they are really good pictures. The poet lampoons the overzealous members of the trade and advises that they be more cautious in their future undertakings to avoid unnecessary mistakes. They should try to curb their greed, which often leads to this overzealousness in the profession.

Veterinary Surgeon

The joy of saving an animal from pain is highlighted in the poem.

Footballer

The wonderful talent of a footballer is celebrated by the poet. The poet emphasises the ingredients that make a good professional footballer: talent, training and hard work, alongside 'the thirst for goals, more goals'. He further celebrates the joy that explodes when each goal is scored. 'My shot like a thunderbolt taking the net apart in unspeakable mechanical daze.'

Milkman

The poet celebrates the wonderful works of a milk vendor and the importance of milk at the cradle of life to man and most animals. He points out how mammals and mothers struggle to breastfeed their young knowing the importance of milk, the white juice of life. He further acknowledges the cow's milk supplement when a mother's milk is inadequate.

Part Three

Selected Poems as Comprehension
Passages

Attempt the following questions:

The Police

1. 'Criminals are cowed at the sight of me.' Who is speaking?

2. 'The world could go to sleep like a baby'. Who is the speaker referring to?

3. How do you think criminals react when they see a police officer?

4. What has the rule of law done to help the police carry out their lawful duties?

5. What happens when you obey the law?

Horticulturist

1. What is a horticulturist's propelling force?

2. What does he blend from pot to pot?

3. What is his stock in trade?

4. What helps to get the best from flowers? Explain.

5. 'Nature's law'. Explain what the poet means by this.

Chef (Caterer)

1. What is like the snow?

2. What are 'reasonably combined', according to the poet?

3. 'Kings and subjects alike are at my beck and call.' Explain.

4. 'Shaking hands with leaders'. What message is the poet trying to convey?

5. 'Clutching my cheque'. Explain.

Medical Doctor (GP)

1. 'Hale and hearty' – whose watchwords are these?

2. 'I can cure ailments.' What message do you think the doctor is trying to put across here?

3. 'Patients must queue to hear my word'. Explain why this must be so.

4. 'An apple every day keeps me away from you.' Explain.

Farmer

1. What is the farmer's ultimate pleasure, according to the poet?

2. What is the first stage of farming?

3. What combines to make a good harvest?

4. 'That journey between the market and home'. What is being referred to here?

5. 'Thanking my tractor for obedience to orders.' Explain.

Pilot

1. According to the poet, what was once a 'mirage'?

2. 'Compass to hand'. What is the function of a compass?

3. 'A little turbulence could ruin it all.' Explain what the poet means. What saves the day from ruin?

4. 'Together we enjoy the mystery of birds in the sky'. Explain what the poet means.

5. 'Of man's dominion over creation'. Explain.

Journalist

1. What is a newshound?

2. 'With papers to <u>scratch</u>'. Replace the underlined word with another word that fits.

3. 'Complex networks, far and near.' Explain.

4. 'Troubled zones are our hot cakes'. Explain what the poet means by this expression.

5. 'We serve it hot'. Explain what is meant by the poet.

Artist

1. 'Semblance structures. My hands conjure.' Explain what the poet means by these statements.

2. Explain 'obeisant to nature'.

Mechanic

1. 'Mechanical intricacies are my crosswords'. Who is being referred to here?

2. Whose job is it to assemble your automobiles?

3. 'Like a physician, I feel their pulse'. Explain.

4. Describe the attire of a mechanic.

5. 'Your computer a drop in the ocean'. Explain.

Miner/Driller

1. What is 'nature's hidden wealth', according to the poet?

2. Where can this 'hidden wealth' be found?

3. 'Hidden out of sight but not out of mind'. Explain.

4. 'Luck on my side, my nation smiles'. Explain the poet's mindset here.

5. 'Touching the numerous lives of the underprivileged'. How could this be?

Lawyer

1. What does the poet say are the lawyer's watchwords?

2. What do you understand by the phrase 'rule of law'?

3. 'Whose ox is gored'. Explain what the poet means here.

4. Explain 'Connection in high places'.

5. 'Our veritable weapon on our battlefield'. Explain.

Fashion Designers

1. 'My clients are lined up'. Who is being referred to here?

2. Explain 'stars storm up'.

3. Explain what the poet means by 'huge sums, huge ideas.'

4. According to the poet, what does he say will make you 'green with envy'?

5. Explain the expression 'Fans fall head over heels as they queue'.

Banker

1. Who is likened to a cricket in October?

2. Describe a banker's outfit as described by the poet.

3. What use is 'accountability' to a banker?

4.	What becomes the banker's propelling force?

5.	What do you understand by the word 'collateral' in this poem?

Postmasters

1.	'Your burden's my burden'. What is being referred to here?

2.	What is not his 'business'?

3.	'My single stride covers the crannies and nooks'. What figure of speech is this?

4.	'News, bitter and sweet'. Explain.

5.	'Cash and kind to better my lot'. Explain.

Sailor

1.	What 'floats on the sea' in this poem?

2.	'My lovely castle with countless cabins'. Explain

3.	'Mingle with the heavens when perceived afar'. Explain.

4.	'Like troublesome children.' What figure of speech is used here?

Salesperson

1. Who is the best of friends to manufacturers?

2. 'Of kinds and brands'. Explain.

3. 'You can bet it, I'll sell coals in Newcastle'. Who is boasting?

4. How does the salesman convince his clients?

5. 'Hooked on my words'. Explain.

Film Actors/Producers

1. What does 'perfection of the arts and of acting' refer to?

2. What does 'script upon script' refer to?

3. What does he do 'all over the world'?

4. What struggles 'in concert to make imagination a reality'?

5. Explain 'Mother Luck smiles on us'.

Athletes (Sprinter)

1. 'My veritable weapons'. Explain.

2. 'Like a hare, I spring to proximity'. What figure of speech is this?

3. What single thought crosses his mind while on the track? Explain.

4. 'Like an eagle's wing'. Explain this figure of speech.

5. What makes doors open for an athlete, according to the poet?

Basketball Player

1. 'Desperate for dunks'. Explain.

2. What do you think gives the basketball player an edge over his peers?

3. Why does he 'fly in the sky'?

4. 'I duck and twist'. Explain.

5. a) 'Charging like an enraged bull'.

    b) 'I hit my target like an archer with a quiverful of arrows'.

    What figure of speech are both of these?

Nurse

1. What is her 'guiding call', according to the poet?

2. 'Never wanting to let them alone'. What does this refer to?

3. What makes the patients 'cry for joy'?

4. Quote the biblical assertion referred to in this poem.

Teacher

1. Who is 'like a potter' according to the poet?

2. According to the poet, what are the following?:

   a) 'potter's wheel';

   b) 'my clay'.

3. Explain the teacher's 'place of emphasis'.

4. Explain 'oldest but newest'.

Singer

1. What do the singer's songs do to the listeners, according to the poet?

2. What touches 'the heart of hearts'? Explain.

3. What does 'my stock in trade' refer to?

4. According to the poet, what do the angels do to the music?

5. According to the poet, who gives the singer her talent?

Clergy

1. According to the poet, what is the clergyman's 'noble call'?

2. Explain the phrase 'nooks and crannies'.

3. Who taught us 'the greatest love of all'?

4. The 'truth the world knew but hated to hear'. Explain.

5. Who is referred to as 'Our Rock of Ages?'

Astronaut

1. According to the poet, what is the astronaut's 'spaceship?'

2. What was covered 'in the twinkling of an eye'? Explain.

3. 'Haven't found courage enough to visit others.' Explain what the poet means by this.

4. Why must the astronaut be 'heavily dressed'?

5. Explain what happens when the astronauts succeed in their mission.

Meteorologist

1. 'My sphere of duty'. Explain.

2. Explain the phrase 'pre-situational idea'.

3. 'I can't be caught with my pants down'. Explain.

4. 'To suit your needs'. Explain.

5. Explain the phrase, 'The weather picks.'

Builder (Civil Engineer)

1. Complex shelters: mansions, towers and skyscrapers'. What does this refer to?

2. Write a short story about what you think builders do.

3. Explain the paraphernalia of a builder.

4. What is the ultimate job of a builder?

5. What are the stages the builder goes though before the work is done?

Firefighter

1. 'Messing up lives and properties'. What is being referred to here?

2. 'Like a stuntman'. Who is being referred to?

3. 'The troubled spot' refers to what?

4. 'Boldly armed'. Explain what the poet means by this.

5. 'We teach fire to steer clear of people's lives'. Explain this.

Carpenter

1. What does 'of varied species' refer to?

2. 'To make my choice'. Explain what choice is being made.

3. What form of uniform does the carpenter wear?

4. What are his work instruments?

5. 'My job beats your imagination'. Explain what the poet means by this.

Dentist

1. What causes damage to teeth, according to the poet?

2. 'Troubled teeth, it's my duty to mend.' Who is speaking?

3. What feeds on our leftovers if we don't brush our teeth?

4. 'Like a baby in its cot.' What figure of speech is this?

5. What 'fights tooth and nail in a bid to damage' teeth?

Secretary

1. 'I know where each is kept.' What is being referred to here?

2. Who is speaking in the poem?

3. What is the function of a barometer?

4. How does the secretary work 'like a watchdog'?

5. Like a computer, I run his outfit'. Explain.

Playwright

1. 'To <u>scratch</u> the paper'. Use another word to replace the underlined word.

2. 'I put characters together in concert'. Explain what the poet means by these words.

3. 'Scripts and speeches it's my calling to write'. Who is speaking?

4. Define the following:

   a) fiction;

   b) non-fiction.

5. Explain what the playwright intends to achieve in his writings, according to the poet.

Shopkeeper

1. 'With a smile on my face'. Use another, similar sentence to replace this one.

2. 'As they troop in and out'. Who is being referred to here?

3. 'Bearing in mind <u>price</u> <u>tags</u>.' Explain what you

understand by the underlined words.

4. What do customers do when they agree to buy a product?

5. 'Basket in hand'. What does this symbolise to a shopper?

Photographer (Paparazzi)

1. 'My daily bread'. Explain what the photographer means by these words.

2. Explain the following:

   a) Industrial and corporate shots;

   b) personal shots.

3. Explain what the poet means by 'solicited or not'.

4. a) How do the photographers act if their target is a superstar?

   b) According to the poet what is their actual reason for doing this?

   c) What is the poet's suggestion as to how this attitude might be avoided?

Veterinary Surgeon

1. According to the poet how does a veterinarian check if an animal is sick?

2. 'Since none can speak a word'. What does this refer to?

3. 'Best of friends to animals, and people's pets.' Who is speaking?

4. How does he help poultry?

5. How does he help the animals' owners?

Carer and Support Worker

1. 'Each time someone knocks at our door'. Whose statement is this?

2. 'Hoping it's true'. Who is being referred to here?

3. 'The greatest challenge of your life'. Explain.

4. 'If we could call it that'. What action is the speaker referring to here?

5. 'Reducing your burden'. Explain.

The British Navy

1. 'Each time we look at you, we cannot but wonder at your source of strength.' What is the poet referring to here?

2. 'this little secret of yours...' Explain what the poet is talking about here.

3. 'Liquid warrior; salty wizards; fighting demons'. What part of speech do you think these are?

4. Mention three benefits of the Royal Navy, according to the poet.

5. What does the poet think is the success behind 'Sea Britain'?

Security Officer

1. 'Your living quarters, my business premises.' Who is speaking?

2. Unwelcome visitors: who are these, according to the writer?

3. 'Like the eagles' what figure of speech is this?

4. What are the security officer's work tools?

5. What does the security officer do to those caught stealing?

The Bin Man

1. 'Your rubbish is mine to clear and sort out'. Who is being referred to here by the writer?

2. Mention the two benefits of the job of a bin man.

3. 'I risk my health'. Who is being referred to here?

4. Mention the two seasons when the bin man works tirelessly, according to the poet?

5. What could have sent millions of people to their early graves if not for the bin man?